Now

Bound

Home

Jenn Johnson-Hamer

Dove and Blackbird Press
Luzerne, PA

Cover design by JJH and Nikki Saltz
Cover image by Canva

Published by
Dove and Blackbird Press
PO Box 13
Luzerne, PA 18709

Library of Congress Control Number: 2022935448

ISBNs:
978-1-957964-00-3 (paperback)
978-1-957964-01-0 (eBook)

These words

Are given in gratitude

Back to the Universe

For its endless springs

Of inspiration

Today…

I am writing. I am thinker, feeling, being.
I am mother. I am wife. I am loved.
I am change. I am transition.
I am carrier of souls.
I am daughter.
I am friend.
I am connection.
I am cognizant. I am sentient. I am all-knowing and kind.
I am goddess personified.
I am power. I am energy.
I am one thousand years of torment. I am release.
I am light and rain and shadow.
I am the dark places from which none return.
I am the dawn of a new day.
I am beginning.
I am
Me.

You were mother
Were you ever mine?
Have we been locked inside
This cycle of birth
Death
Lather, rinse
Repeat

Could we begin again
After all we've lost
To time's elusive seductress
Tempting us again and again
To surrender to the cycle of birth
Death
Lather, rinse
Repeat

Now I wait
Spirit moves in me
Body a breath behind
This babe held inside
This cycle of birth
Death
Lather, rinse
Repeat

I wait.
I whimper.
I wish.
I weep.
It burns.
It tears.
It festers.
It seeps.
It changes.
It grows.
It evolves.
It gives.
I heal.
I recover.
I discover.

I live.

Inside this body
Do two hearts dwell
One's come from heaven
While one's been through hell
And inside the bones
Will the truth be found
Of just who we are
And how we are bound

One night we met as lovers do
My heart exploded, swelled
Only to find I'd been left behind
As you dove headfirst into hell
My drowning lungs gasped for air
As my lips sealed up shut tight

Now I watch unfolding presently

…My life begin that night

The ache
The pulse
The missing
A phantom limb
Torn asunder

Still feeling the pain
I let you in

You are of me
In me
With me

To part is to leave
Unknown
A shard of my soul
In your possession

Until it is returned
To its rightful place
It shall scream of its loss

Banging its head
Against my ribs
Until you come home
Again

I shrink
From that which I do not wish to touch
A poison
A toxin
At once encircling my dipped-in toe
The virus that will kill me
And lay waste to all I have become

I am between
Pressed
Stone
The air delicately wrung from my lungs
Like icing piped to the last sweet grain

I am forgotten
Whispered
Sand
My being freshly swatted from the air
Like gnats swarming in the summer sun

And then…

I am free
Dancing
Bliss
The air rushing in lungs expand I can breathe I can breathe
I can breathe I can breathe
Like the tide releasing into the crystal waters

I am seen

You are my adventure
My co-explorer and my heart
I will journey with you anywhere
Even valleys of the dark
We don't need a destination
Like the magi, just a star
For the greatest magic lies within
Simply being where we are

My poetry pours
From ink to page
From formless to the form
It is
Of rounded edges
And sharp teeth
Of pain and fortune
Of memory

Of forgetting

I am
But a slave
To the mess
It leaves
On my pages
And the linens
It has left behind
For me to clean

My heart can love
In every color
Sing
In every song
Can move and dance
Within another
And know
Where it belongs

My heart is not
Restricted by
Law or time
Or fear
But swells to welcome
Every cry
And know
They matter here

I have an addiction
To connection
A rare faction
Of the human condition
I crave relation
In every action
And seek creation
With unbridled passion

Listen to the rain
Tap tapping
On the roof
Soaking in every grain
Every nail
And every tooth
Swelling with the volume
Of its sorrow
And its mirth
Cleansing us of all our doom
And guiding us
To birth

Breathe
Breathe
Breathe
Release
Calm
Soothe
Tame
The Beast
Breathe
Breathe
Breathe
Let go
Placid
Quiet
Winter Snow
Breathe
Breathe
Breathe
Extend
Inward
Outward
In Again
Breathe
Breathe
Breathe
Relax
Victor
Over
This Attack

Memories linger
Like fine wisps of silk
Weaving her web
For my foolish design
Again and again
I fall under her spell
Her threads entwine me
A willing prey
Down, down, down she goes
Smoothly spinning beyond my reach
I surrender to her will
Blissful

Until

That first fatal bite

I see inside your head, my love
I see inside your fear
I see your walls made far too high
To climb, break down, or clear

Until you stop pretending
Who is welcome and who falls
You will remain afraid and stuck
You'll never love
At all

Grab your sabre
Take a poke
See how many
Fires you stoke
Slice and cut
Fix the game
From your view
We're all the same
Bend the knee
Consent to chains
Up on your throne
O'er us you reign

I –

I am certainly
Not perfection
I am hardly
Even convention
Sick to death
Of your pretension
Keeping me
In this detention
Begging for
Your ripe attention
As I fight
This growing tension
To live within
My own dimension
And moving toward
My soul's ascension

I take each word
And I swallow it down
Swallow it down
Swallow it down
The taste
Bitter
Bittersweet
Longing
For truth
That could make me free
But I swallow it down
Swallow it down
Swallow it down
For you
Your ease
Your peace of mind
My tongue dry
Throat parched
With the earth
Crumbling
And I swallow it down
Swallow it down
Swallow it down
Knowing nothing that I do
Will ever be
Good enough
For you

What is a king
Who extorts his crown
As peasants
And passers-by
Are held to the ground
No leader is he
Who demands respect
"With love"
As he tightens
The noose 'round your neck
Tyranny
Is not justice
Is not love
Or concern
But the wish
Of a ruler
Who would watch
The world
Burn

I want to write a poem about love
But what can be said that hasn't been said
How your hands care for my every need
Your ears hear my every word
Your eyes see my every flaw

And your heart loves every anyway

I want to write a poem about love
I want to say what hasn't been said
How your shoulder is my safety
Your lap my comfort
Your nose my delight

And your heart loves every anyway

But you are love personified
None of my words can ever touch
The glory that is you

You are a poem about love
You are all that has been said and not said
How your body gives in every move
Your lips in every breath
Your soul in every word and deed

And my heart loves every anyway

Within my womb
There is a babe
Who will one day
Lay at my breast
In this alone
I place my faith
My life is this
And fuck the rest

My love,
I hope you're proud of me
Of all I've endured
How far I've come

What it will mean
To hold you in my arms
This perfect creation
This bliss
I have been moving toward
My whole life

You

My beautiful one
You were the key all along
The part that was
Never quite whole

I never knew
I was waiting for you
In every struggle
In every release

In every decision to live

You were my destiny
I was your choice
And together
We will make
The greatest
Magic

What a poignant place to be
Here observing history
As in our eyes it's plain to see
Instead of reading what they claim to be
In order to spin
Our reality

May I be made
Into the image
Spirit has for me
And more importantly
The image that
I have for myself

I create my own reality
I speak miracles into existence

What does it matter
If I do declare
My faith
My stance
My sex
My hair
I will always be seen
Just how you choose
My race
My gender
My height
My shoes
I know me
And that is imperative
My heart
My soul
My hopes
My narrative
So I will continue
To live in this me-dom
My breath
My life
My joy
My freedom

I am
My reason for being

You are
My reason
For believing

Intimidate
Procreate
Insulate
Obliterate
Exacerbate
Confiscate
Demonstrate
Generate
Indicate
Integrate
Estimate
Emulate
Mediate
Separate
Segregate
All your hate

Who am I

Do you know me

Have you met me before

Do you only see
Your own projections
Expectations
Failures

Have you ever really come to know
The me that stands
In front of you

Built on truth

Not just perception

Living
Breathing
Existing
Thriving

Are you threatened

That I have my own mind
My own life
My own struggles

My own success

I appreciate your guidance
But do not mistake me
For a child

For I have grown

So much taller

Than you

All we like sheep
Are led by day
Forever wandering
Astray
Each content
In his own way
To believe
In this decay
Of every single word
They say
Vow each injustice
We'll repay

When all you had to do
…was stay

Your inability
To grow
Does not necessitate
My requirement
To stop

A butterfly does not question the dark
But rests within it until she is free
To dance
To fly
To soar
In her newly-formed wings

If you are the highway
Then I am the lines
Guiding you safely
And helping you
Always
To move forward

The line of our femininity
Traced back through generations
Of my mother's mother's mother
And beyond
Broken
A cancer in our souls
Doomed to lament through generations
Until the light
That is my own
Shines forth to guide us all
Into tomorrow
Of me and my mother
Of my mother's mother's mother
And beyond
Healed

My breath, it is a temple
My blood, it is the wine
That flows in truth abundant
Forever only mine

I stand within my energy
Reclaiming what I'd lost
Renewed, reborn unto myself
I am divinely wrought

Who among us can say

I AM

And mean it

I am
The carrier of souls
The mother
Whose arms one day will hold
The daughter
In whom the world holds faith
The soul
Whose breath will forever create

Echoes
Echoes of ten
Of ten hundred
Of ten thousand
Years
Lives
Generations
All pulsing
Beating
Meeting
To create me
Here
Echoes of time
Of distance
Of memory
Echoes don't forget
And I
I am the symbol
The channel
The proof
That life still goes on
That strength
Courage
Perseverance
Matter
That healing
Is worth it
That we
Are in charge
Of our own destiny
Guided by Spirit
By One
By All
To place our feet
Exactly where they
Are supposed to be

May we all find the peace
Of a gentle rain
On lily stone
And a firefly's kiss
Goodnight

Author's Note

I have been writing poetry since childhood. I remember offering some to an English class or two and being judged, harshly, for it by my peers.

As a songwriter, it was easier to have my words taken more seriously. Coupled with a memorable melody, no one felt the need to pry it apart or sneer at its content.

I stopped writing poetry for decades. But being homebound during a pandemic, pregnant, surrounded by rising social tensions, I found that my inclination was to return to my roots. And thus, poetry found its way back to my hand.

This chapbook was originally a submission for a poetry contest. And while I didn't win, I am grateful to it for pushing me to take the leap and turn my notebook scribblings into something more. Dozens of poems did not make the cut, but I am already working on a second volume that will be a broader spectrum of inner workings I'd like to share.

I look forward to meeting you there.

Wishing you peace.

~ JJH

Acknowledgements

For those of you who are unfamiliar with the phenomenon, putting your work out there is terrifying. So anyone who helps quell the bottomless well of fear deserves some recognition for it.

First, thank you to Kaylene, for always giving me feedback no matter what. To Halle for her initial insights. And to both of you for being my favorite part about my writing process – our evenings spent brainstorming and workshopping. Thank you both for being such a great support system through everything.

Thank you to Nikki for your guidance and assistance with my beautiful cover.

Thank you to Michele for your openness and support.

Thank you to my mother for being the source of inspiration for a few of these poems, and for babysitting duty so my kiddo was cared for while I was getting some much needed work done.

Thank you to Tom and Cady for being my muses, my love, my reasons for going on, and for always believing in me.

Thank you to all of you who have chosen to support this work. I hope you have found something you needed within its words.

And thank you to my past self, for getting to this point. For not letting fear win. For staying the course and trusting the magic. I hope I've made you proud.

About the Author

Author photo credit: Amanda Duffy

Jenn Johnson-Hamer lives in a small town in the northeast with her husband and daughter, and their cat. She can often be found working or chatting in local coffee and ice cream shops.

www.ingramcontent.com/pod-product-compliance
Lightning Source LLC
Chambersburg PA
CBHW061326120626
46546CB00007B/2695